The New Church Kneeler Book

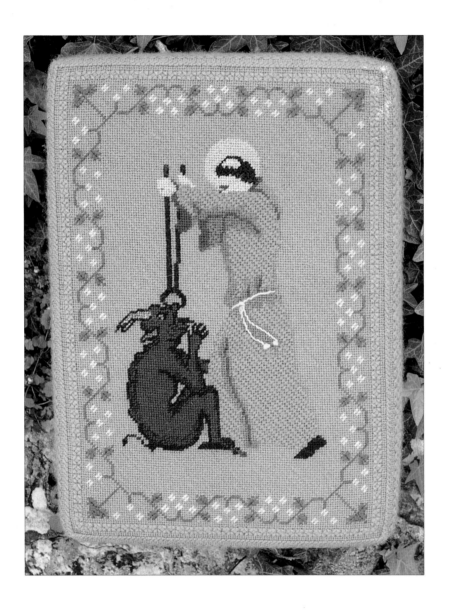

THE NEW CHURCH KNEELER BOOK

ANGELA DEWAR

SEARCH PRESS

First published in Great Britain 1997

Search Press Limited
Wellwood, North Farm Road,
Tunbridge Wells, Kent TN2 3DR

ISBN 0 85532 825 8

Suppliers
If you have any difficulty in obtaining any of the materials or equipment mentioned in this book, then please write for a current list of stockists, including firms who operate a mail-order service, to the Publishers:
Search Press Limited, Wellwood,
North Farm Road, Tunbridge Wells,
Kent TN2 3DR, England

Printed in Spain by Elkar S. Coop. Bilbao 48012

I would like to thank the following, for their various contributions to this book:
Ann Bains
Gisela Banbury
Rosemary Lowery
Dr Ken Nott
Beatrice Perry
Phyllis Richardson
Sara Stonor
Jennifer Stuart
The Craft Collection, Paterna Yarns
Winchester Cathedral, the Dean and Chapter

I would also like to thank the following for lending kneelers:
St Augustine's Chapel, Tonbridge School, Kent
St Bartholomew's Church, Burwash, Sussex
St Dunstan's Church, Mayfield, Sussex
St John the Baptist's Church, Penshurst, Kent
St John the Evangelist's Church, Hildenborough, Kent
St John's Methodist Church, Southborough, Kent
St Mary's Church, Speldhurst, Kent
St Nicholas' Church, Sevenoaks, Kent
St Peter and St Paul's Church, Tonbridge, Kent

With special thanks to St Dunstan's Church, Mayfield, Sussex and St Nicholas' Church, Sevenoaks, Kent for allowing the Publishers to visit their churches to photograph some of the kneelers featured in this book.

PAGE 1
This kneeler is taken from a set that appears in St Dunstan's Church, Mayfield, Sussex (see pages 34–35). It features St Dunstan resisting the devil with a pair of blacksmith's tongs. The kneeler was designed by Anne Adam and Gillian Elvy and is worked in Appleton's crewel wool using a wide variety of stitches.

PAGE 3
This beautiful kneeler is from St Bartholomew's Church in Burwash, Sussex (see pages 40–41), and features a pair of birds. It was designed by the late Barbara Newton and worked by Elsie Taylor using tent stitch, back stitch, cross stitch, rice stitch and Gobelin.

OPPOSITE
Deer from Knole Park in Sevenoaks, form the theme for this kneeler, which is part of a set in St Nicholas' Church in Sevenoaks, Kent (see pages 38–39). The deer are both worked in tent stitch.

Contents

Introduction

The hassocks or kneelers of most parish churches in the past were simple padded supports designed to make kneeling down during services more comfortable. They were functional items, covered with plain and durable fabrics such as baize, serge, leather or plush. In 1930, Louisa Pesel revolutionised the design of these hassocks when she organised the first kneeler scheme at Winchester Cathedral. For the next six years, under her guidance, the Winchester Broderers worked cushions and kneelers for the Cathedral. Louisa Pesel drew her designs from historical sources, including embroidered samplers from the seventeenth century. From these, she adapted floral motifs and made use of interlacing bands combined with rondels, some containing ships featured in the Bayeux Tapestry; these were stitched from watercolours painted by Sybil Blunt.

The decoration of church kneelers became more popular after the Second World War, when many churches needed rebuilding and refurnishing, and when embroidery materials became available again. Today, many hundreds of churches own embroidered kneelers. Some have kneelers which have been specially made for the clergy or important visitors, but the majority are designed to be used by the congregation. The designs range from religious symbols and images, to contemporary scenes of modern living and city life, and they often complement the architecture and design of the church interior.

Four cushions from Winchester Cathedral, designed by Louisa Pesel and worked by the Winchester Broderers between 1930 and 1936, using wool stitched on canvas.

There are five main types of kneeler used today. The standard cushion is used by the congregation in the main body of the church, and it usually measures 35 x 25 x 8cm (14 x 10 x 3in). The deep pad or hassock is considerably higher than the standard cushion, being 15–23cm (6–9in) deep, and it may also be larger than the standard rectangular size. It is more suitable for elderly members of the congregation, and it has 'ears' on each side which are used for lifting. The box kneeler is a wooden box with a sloping, padded and hinged lid, sometimes found in old churches. The stool kneeler comprises a wooden stool with a sloping, padded top, upholstered with embroidered canvas. The long kneeler is usually designed for special places or occasions and it can be any size.

Clear step-by-step photographs are included in this book to guide you through the whole process of embroidering and making up a kneeler for a church or chapel. It is an enjoyable process, whether you work alone or as part of an organised group, and I hope that with the help of this book, you will soon be able to create your own original designs.

Materials and tools

The materials and tools needed for making a church kneeler are all readily available at needlecraft and craft suppliers. In the picture opposite, design materials, yarns and needles are shown. The tools, canvasses and frames required are shown on pages 10–13.

Yarns

Church kneelers are traditionally worked on canvas and the yarns for this type of canvas work should be of good quality. They are available in several thicknesses and textures and in many different colours. The types most often used are shown opposite. There are several makes of tapestry and crewel wools which have been developed specifically for embroidery and will not become roughened during use. Crewel wool is thinner than tapestry wool and several strands may be used together. The yarn should cover the canvas but not distort it. Other yarns may be used to add interest to the surface. Stranded cottons, silk and pearl yarns of a suitable thickness may be used to provide sheen and highlights, and a small quantity of metallic thread can be used to add richness. Extra-strong thread should be used when making up the kneeler (see page 32).

Needles

Tapestry needles are used for canvas embroidery and are available in a variety of sizes. Use one that is large enough to thread comfortably, but not so large that it will distort the canvas as it goes through the holes – this is important, as there are many stitches where one hole is used several times. A large, strong, sharp needle or a curved needle should be used when making up the kneeler (see page 32).

Scissors

Dressmaker's scissors are used for the canvas, and embroidery scissors for the yarn. Curved nail scissors are useful for cutting threads close to the canvas.

Other items

A soft (2B) pencil and a sketch book can be used to record any design ideas. A pencil can also be used to mark the size of the foam block on to the calico wrapping during the making up process (see page 31). Use either a waterproof marker pen or acrylic paint and a fine paint brush to transfer designs on to the canvas surface (see page 18). You will need strong pins when making up the kneeler, and you may also find a pin cushion useful. When you come to stretch the finished embroidery, you will need a board together with a colour-fast towel (see page 29). Finally, you will need a D-ring if the kneeler is to hang in the pew.

OPPOSITE

1. Pure silk yarn
2. Tapestry wool, crewel wool, Paterna Persian wool
3. Pearl cotton
4. Waterproof marker pens
5. Extra-strong thread
6. Tapestry needles, size 18–24, and large, strong, sharp needle
7. Pins and pin cushion
8. Sketch book
9. D-rings
10. Embroidery scissors
11. 2B pencils
12. Acrylic paint
13. Paint brush
14. Eraser
15. Stranded cottons
16. Coton à broder

Canvas

Use the best quality canvas available. The majority of canvas is made from linen or cotton. A canvas with a 'lock' on the weft threads, known as interlock canvas, will not distort when it is embroidered and it will keep its shape well when being worked.

Single-thread canvas is more versatile because a larger variety of stitches can be worked over it. Double-thread canvas is suitable for cross stitch and tent stitch. On double canvas, large background stitches can be combined with small stitches for more detailed work – divide the pairs of warp and weft threads with a large needle and treat selected areas as a single canvas. The different scales can enliven a design.

A selection of different canvases

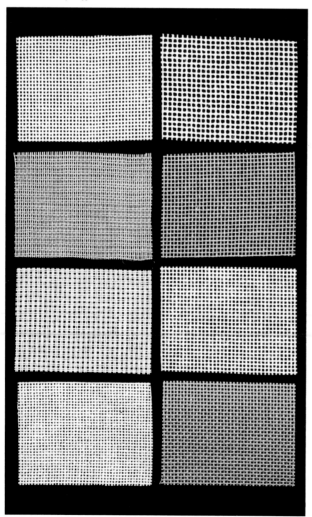

Fabrics

Several fabrics are used in the making up of kneelers. Domette is laid underneath the canvas to provide extra padding on top of the cushion; a block of foam is covered with calico and inserted into the canvas shape – the foam must be the high-density type or the kneeler will not provide enough support; tarpaulin hessian is used to back the underside of the kneeler; webbing tape is used to attach the D-ring to the calico-covered pad; and wadding can be used to fill the corners if the foam does not fit perfectly into the canvas.

Materials and tools for framing

Canvas is easier to work on if it is fixed to a frame (see pages 12–15). You can use staples or drawing pins to secure the canvas to a simple wooden frame; use pliers to remove them once the embroidery is finished.

If you are lacing the canvas to a frame, use strong upholsterer's thread. This is also used to lace the canvas around the foam filling.

OPPOSITE

1. Wadding	9. Dressmaker's scissors
2. Frame	10. Staple gun
3. Canvas	11. Hammer
4. Masking tape	12. Drawing pins
5. Webbing tape	13. Calico
6. Upholsterer's thread	14. Pliers
7. Domette	15. High-density foam
8. Tarpaulin hessian	

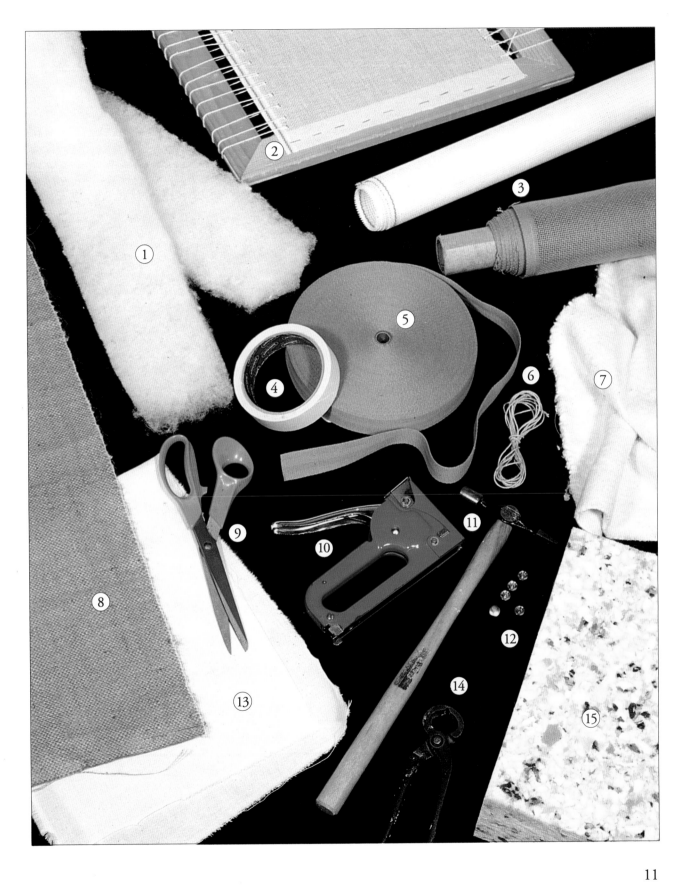

Frames and framing

Canvas embroidery can be held in the hand and worked, but it is easier and quicker to work on a canvas that is stretched over a frame. Stretching the canvas on a frame means that the finished embroidery is less likely to be distorted, and so it will be much simpler to make up into a well-shaped kneeler.

A selection of frames is shown opposite.

A wooden floor frame has the advantage of leaving both hands free to embroider, which means that work can progress quickly. The frame can be swung to a vertical position when it is not in use.

A slate frame held by a steel post and clamp has all the advantages of the floor frame but it takes up much less space. It is also more stable than the wooden frame, and it is more versatile, as the clamp will support almost any size of frame.

A travel frame is useful if you are working during a journey. It is easily portable, but the disadvantages are that you are unable to see the whole design at once, and the canvas needs to be re-rolled from time to time.

An artist's canvas stretcher makes an economical, easy-to-use frame for a pew kneeler. The four sides of the frame slot into each other and the canvas may be pinned, laced or stapled to it. Stretchers may be obtained in many sizes from artist's suppliers.

A home-made frame is needed if you are working on an unusual shape, such as the one shown in the photograph opposite which is longer than usual. The canvas can be fixed to the frame with a combination of staples and lacing.

A home-made frame can be made cheaply from four pieces of strong wood, screws and angle brackets, as shown above. Check that the corners are square before securing them. The frame must form a true rectangle and be rigid when assembled.

A home-made frame

Framing-up the canvas

No matter what type of frame or method of attachment is chosen, the canvas must be tightly stretched and have the threads running in straight lines.

Using a slate, travel or floor frame

If you are using a slate, travel or floor frame, follow the step-by-step instructions below to attach the canvas to the frame.

TIP

Since only short side lengths are exposed when working on a narrow travel frame, it is not always necessary to lace the sides.

1. Use a tape measure to find the centre of the webbing on both rollers, and the centre of both long edges of the canvas. Mark the centres.

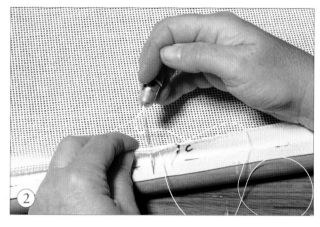

2. Fold over a 1cm ($\frac{1}{2}$in) hem and match the centre of the canvas to the centre of the webbing on one roller. Oversew the two edges together, working from the centre to the corners. Repeat on the other roller.

3. Insert the side pieces of the frame. Tighten the tension following the manufacturer's instructions. Here, the inner nuts are tightened towards the outer ones to make the canvas taut.

4. Cut 2.5m (1$\frac{3}{4}$yd) of string or lacing thread. Thread a carpet needle and tie the end on to the side arm of the frame. Lace the canvas with lacing stitches approximately 1.5cm ($\frac{3}{4}$in) apart. Repeat on the other side.

Using a home-made frame or an artist's stretcher

To staple or pin canvas on to an artist's stretcher or a home-made frame, begin by cutting the canvas to the outer dimensions of the frame. Staple or pin the canvas to the wood, starting at the centre of the top and bottom rails and working out towards the corners. Repeat on the two side rails.

The canvas may also be laced on to an artist's stretcher or a home-made frame. To do this, cut the canvas 1cm smaller than the inner dimensions of the frame. Stitch string or extra-strong thread through the canvas and around the frame, working from the centre of the top rail to one corner. Fix the lacing thread to the corner by winding it around a drawing pin or secure it with sticky tape. Work to the other corner in the same way. Lace the opposite side and then the two remaining sides in the same way. When you have finished, tighten up the lacing if the canvas feels slack.

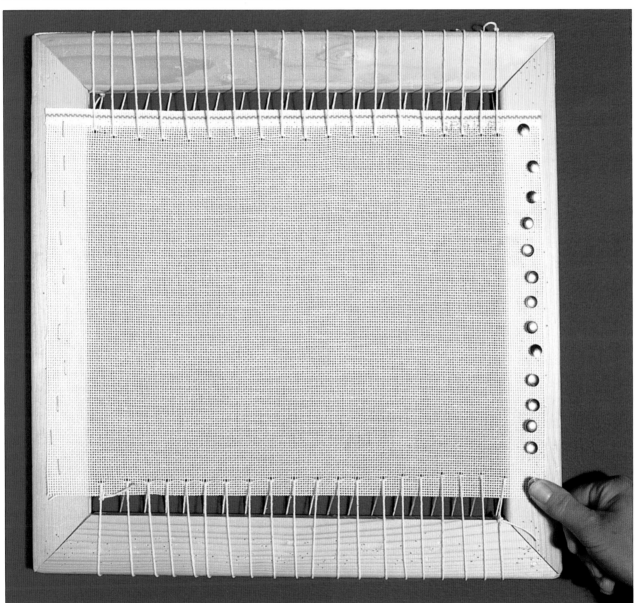

This picture shows the different ways in which canvas can be secured to an artist's stretcher or a home-made frame. You can use drawing pins, staples, or the canvas can be laced on to the sides.

Design

A good design should have meaning as well as aesthetic charm. You do not have to look far for inspiration for a design – the Bible, Christian history, church architecture and interior furnishings all provide plenty of ideas. A simple well-executed design is often more successful than one which is complex and over-ambitious, so choose the subject carefully.

The kneeler you make may well be displayed alongside many others, so select the colours with this in mind. If a church is to be furnished with a whole new set of kneelers, it is easier to be a little more adventurous with colour schemes, but an individually worked kneeler has to harmonise with established colours. Each kneeler should not only complement its neighbour, but it should also enhance the church interior. Consider the colours of permanent fixtures such as stained glass windows, floor tiles, or stone and brickwork. Existing carpet and upholstery colours should also be taken into account.

Developing a design

The transition from sketch to stitched design is something which some people find difficult. Once you have decided on a subject, experiment with your sketches to see how to best arrange them to create a strong design. There are lots of different ways to work with a single subject; the photographs opposite show how grapes can be used in a variety of ways.

Kneelers at St Nicholas' Church, Sevenoaks, Kent. The colours have been chosen to harmonize with and complement the architecture and interior of the church.

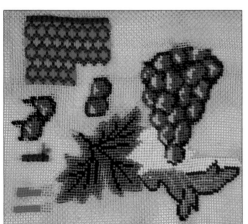

TOP LEFT

This rough sketch of a vine has been the starting point for several of my designs, including the one featured in the project on pages 26–33.

MIDDLE LEFT

Beatrice Perry's original trials for the kneeler scheme at St Peter and St Paul's Church in Tonbridge, Kent.

BOTTOM LEFT

This beautiful kneeler is the central communion kneeler at St Peter and St Paul's Church in Tonbridge, Kent. The fleur-de-lys pattern and the cross are taken from the encaustic tiles in the church, which were designed by Pugin. The pictures in the lozenges are derived from biblical reference. The lozenge motifs are designed by Debbie Noble and the borders by Beatrice Perry. Appleton crewel wool is used and the stitches are mainly tent and single cross stitch. The wheat ears are a variation of leaf stitch.

RIGHT

A hand-painted Victorian pattern of a grape vine, designed especially for Berlin woolwork which was so popular during the nineteenth century.

Transferring a design

You can copy an existing design and then transfer it to the canvas, but I prefer to make my own designs, after researching a particular subject and the church environment. Whatever the source of your motifs, you will need to arrange them into a pattern that will fit the top of your kneeler. The best and easiest way to do this, is to enlarge or reduce them on a photocopier. You can then experiment with sizes and positions until you are satisfied with your design. Now follow the instructions below to transfer the design on to the canvas.

1. Copy out your design on to plain white paper using a pencil.

TIP

You can sketch your design straight on to paper or paste elements of it on to paper and then take a photocopy of the final design.

Use a waterproof pen or waterproof paint to transfer the design on to the canvas, as the embroidery will be damp-stretched when it is finished.

If you are using pale colours for the embroidery, use a pale acrylic paint rather than a dark marker pen to transfer the design.

If you make a mistake while you are working, use correction fluid to cover it.

2. Use a dark felt-tip pen to go over the drawing to make the image more pronounced.

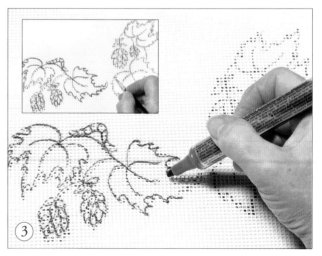
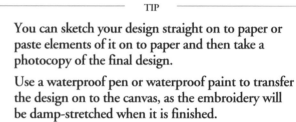

3. Tape the design to the table, then lay the canvas over it. Match the centre of the design with the centre of the canvas, then tape the canvas over the design. Mark the design on to the canvas using either a permanent marker pen or acrylic paint and a fine brush.

These cushions were designed and made by Angela Dewar and Pat Prior for St John's Methodist Church, Southborough, Kent. The designs are based on local themes, and the border of hop leaves and flowers includes a small insect which is found in local hopfields. The stitches include tent, Gobelin, brick, upright cross and a grounding pattern of satin stitches and tent stitch. Appleton crewel wool is used for the embroidery and highlights are worked in silk.

Stitches

Tent stitch, which can be worked horizontally or diagonally, and cross stitch are the most familiar of the canvas work stitches, but there are many other stitches that can be used to create lively and interesting patterns and textures. The simple stitches featured here have been chosen because they lie in relatively short lengths on the surface of the canvas. Long, straggly stitches are not robust enough to withstand constant wear and will often snag during use.

Modern, lightweight kneelers are often hung up in the pews when not in use. This exposes the sides of the kneelers, and so textured stitches can be used to decorate borders and edges. To cover the canvas, straight stitches should be worked in a thicker yarn than slanting or crossed stitches. Try to work an even, but not too tight tension and when the embroidery is completed, check on the reverse side that all thread ends are secure.

Whatever stitches you use, remember that the top of the kneeler must be comfortable and that highly raised or rough-textured stitches will be painful on the knees!

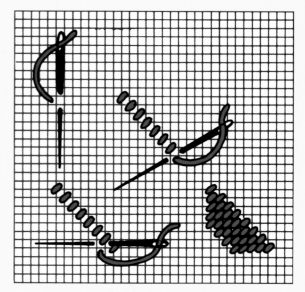

diagonal tent stitch

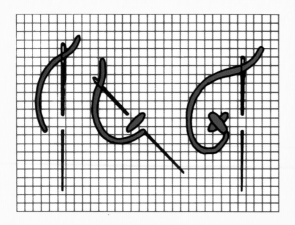

cross stitch

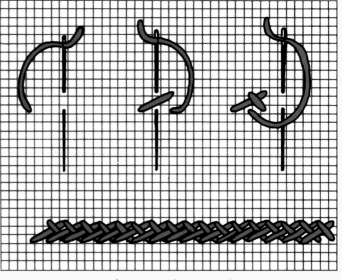

long-armed cross stitch

20

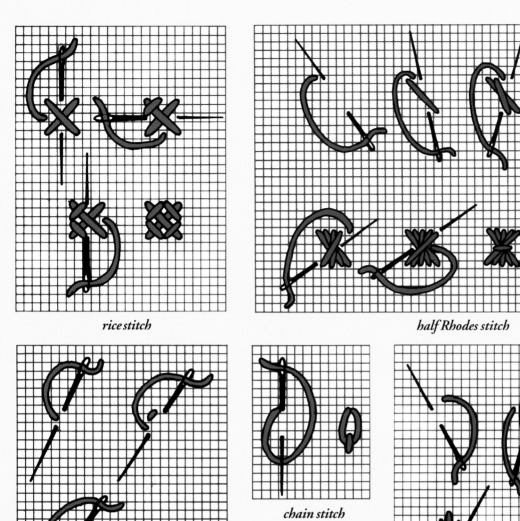

rice stitch

half Rhodes stitch

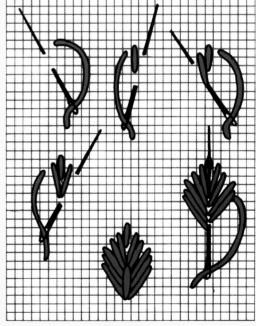

satin stitch square

chain stitch

leaf stitch

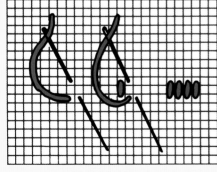

A selection of simple stitches suitable for canvaswork.

Gobelin stitch

21

Border designs

Canvaswork stitches can be combined to make wonderful, rich borders. Even two very simple stitches can make interesting and exciting patterns. A border can be used to decorate the sides of a kneeler or to frame a design on the top. If the border is going on top of the kneeler, the four corners must be neatly designed. This presents more of a challenge to the designer, as the pattern must be counted out carefully to fit into the given space and over the correct number of threads. The photograph opposite shows a group of six patterns, ranging from simple to quite complex. Details of some of the stitches used are shown on pages 20–21.

The home-made long frame shown on page 13, shows a very free way of designing a 'frame' border. This design of hop leaves and hops is used on a set of kneelers and cushions in St John's Methodist Church in Southborough, Kent; in this way, the central space is left clear for other symbols. The border has the effect of linking all the kneelers. Four of the kneelers are oddly shaped at one end because they form a mitred corner around the communion rail steps, so the design is made to fit into this shape. Other unusual shaped kneelers with interesting border patterns can be found on pages 16 and 36.

OPPOSITE

1. A trial border for the communion kneelers at St Peter and St Paul's Church, Tonbridge, Kent, using long satin stitch, tent stitch and Gobelin stitch. The completed border can be seen on page 17.

2. A simple but effective border and corner using only two stitches – long satin stitch and diamond eyelet.

Designed by Beatrice Perry

3. An arrangement of leaf stitches in two colours on a background of tent stitch. The edges are in Gobelin stitch, with details in upright cross, and the leaf stems are worked in gold metallic thread.

4. A mixture of tent stitch, Gobelin stitch, half Rhodes stitch, rice stitch and satin stitch square combine to make this attractive textured pattern.

5. A simple corner pattern of satin stitch squares in stranded cotton with an overlay of yellow silk, and an edging of double cross stitch and tent stitch worked in wool.

Designed by Angela Dewar

6. A complex border corner pattern based on a variation of cross stitches, with edges in satin stitch square, Gobelin and tent stitch. The details are in metallic thread.

Designed by Gisela Banbury

A border from the side of a kneeler from the Galilee Chapel in Durham Cathedral, designed by the Reverend Leonard Childs.

Using charts

Some designs are available already drawn out on to squared graph paper. Details such as colour, type of stitches and background areas, are usually clearly marked on these patterns. You can work these designs straight from the chart on to the canvas, without marking it out. The centre of the design should be marked on the chart; this will be the first stitch, and it should be worked in the exact centre of the canvas. Thereafter, all stitches must be counted out. People who find this process difficult, may prefer a design drawn directly on to the canvas (see page 18).

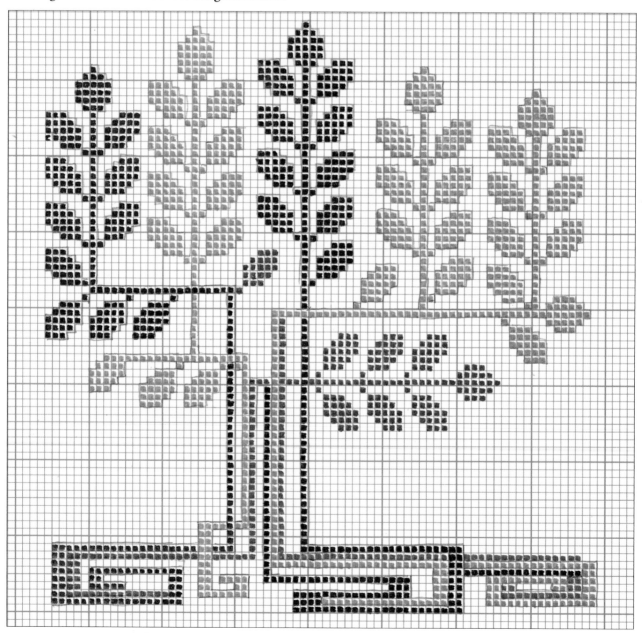

This Tree of Life was designed and worked by Gisela Banbury, using tapestry yarn and tent stitch on a single canvas. It is shown here without a background, for clarity. There are many stitches which would be suitable for creating an interesting and textured surface as a backing for the design – satin stitch square is one possibility. This tree would make an excellent central motif for a kneeler and surrounding it with a border pattern would enrich the design further.

Wheat and vine kneeler

This simple project is worked mainly in diagonal tent stitch and it shows all the stages that go into making up a kneeler. The design is for a standard cushion (see page 6) and it is suitable for a church of any denomination. The symbols of the Holy Communion are common to many Christian Faiths. The wheat ears on either side of the central stem are bent over reflecting the words of Christ: 'This is my body, broken for you.' Jesus also said: 'I am the true vine', so these symbols are known and understood by Christians everywhere.

The background colour may be changed to fit into any colour scheme, and you could also choose to decorate the plain sides with a border pattern if you wish (see page 22).

This project uses Paterna Persian wool which is three-stranded and loosely twisted. Two strands are needed to cover a twelve-thread canvas working in diagonal tent stitch. Colours may be mixed in the needle to add interest.

To start

Enlarge the design shown opposite on a photocopier by 175%. Transfer the full-size pattern on to the canvas using dark red waterproof pen or acrylic paint to match the background colour (see page 18). Frame up the canvas (see pages 14–15).

To start stitching, make a knot in the end of a two-strand length of yarn. Cut your yarn no longer than 40cm (16in), or it will wear thin. Insert your needle into the front of the canvas, about 4cm (1½in) from your starting point, which should always be the centre of the canvas. The knot remains on the surface of the canvas until you have worked in the thread on the back with your stitching; it may then be cut off. Finish off in the same way; leave the tail of thread on the front until the back is secure, then cut it off. This method avoids spoiling the tension of the front of the work caused by darning into the back. However, the final thread will have to be darned in, so try to plan for it to be in an inconspicuous position.

You will need

Canvas, 50 x 65cm (20 x 25in), 12 threads to every 2.5cm (1in)

Paterna Persian wool:
  1 skein Nos. 692, 693 and 694, loden green
  1 skein Nos. 311 and 312, grape
  2 hanks No. D211, antique rose
  2 skeins No. 727, autumn yellow
  1 skein No. 732, honey gold

Anchor stranded cotton:
  1 skein No. 108, light mauve

High-density foam, 35 x 25 x 8cm (14 x 10 x 3in)

Domette, 35 x 25cm (14 x 10in)

Calico, 56 x 71cm (22 x 28in)

Tarpaulin hessian, 42 x 32cm (17 x 13in)

D-ring

Webbing tape, approximately 120cm (47in) long, 2.5cm (1in) wide

Polyester wadding (a handful)

Upholsterer's lacing thread

Extra-strong thread

Needles

Board (slightly larger than the canvas)

Masking tape

Colour-fast towel

Rust-proof drawing pins

Small hammer

The design for the wheat and vine kneeler

The embroidery

The kneeler is worked in diagonal tent stitch, with the exception of the ears of wheat which are worked in chain, and the tendrils which are worked in tent stitch. Begin in the centre with the wheat, and use honey gold to work the stems, leaves and ears. Use autumn yellow to stitch the outline of the chalice then fill in the centre.

Work the leaf veins with honey gold, then stitch the leaves using three shades of loden green. Begin at the outer edges with the darkest green, and gradually blend the colours towards the centres, ending up with the lightest shade. Use two different colours in the needle to produce a subtle colour change.

Stitch the grapes in two shades of grape. Use the dark shade on the left edge and the light shade in the remaining area. Leave three to five stitches on each grape empty; stitch in highlights using six strands of light mauve Anchor stranded cotton.

Stitch the stems and tendrils using a pale loden green. Count out the stitches and work one side first. Stitch the other side as a mirror image. Do not worry if the curves do not match each other exactly.
Work the background in diagonal tent stitch using antique rose. Remember to leave two empty threads of canvas around the top of the kneeler. Finish off the last stitch by turning the canvas over on to the wrong side and darning in the end of the yarn.

Here I show several motifs worked. I have started in the centre of the design and stitched the outlines first, before filling them in. It does not matter in which order the motifs are worked, but it is essential that the background is embroidered last. Remember to leave two empty threads around the edge of the top of the kneeler. These will be covered during the making up of the kneeler (see page 30, step 3).

Working the background

Darning in the yarn

The back of the embroidered kneeler, ready for stretching.

28

Stretching the canvas

Stretching improves the appearance of canvas embroidery and also helps to reshape a distorted canvas. It may be done professionally but it is not difficult to do at home.

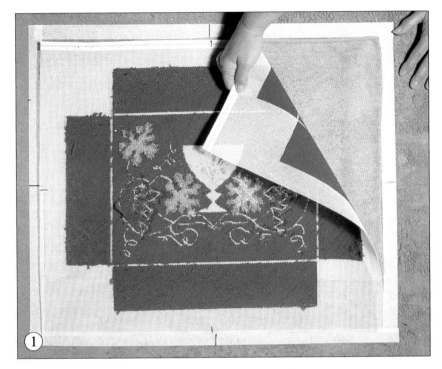

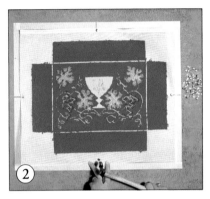

2. Match and secure the centre points of the canvas to those on the board using rust-proof drawing pins. Stretch the canvas as tightly as you can and work from top to bottom and from the centre outwards to secure it to the board.

1. Use masking tape to mark out a square on the board the same size as your canvas. Ensure that the angles are perfectly square. Mark the middle centre of each side. Place a wet colour-fast towel on top of the board, then put the canvas face down on top of the towel.

TIP

Choose a board soft enough for drawing pins to be fixed into.

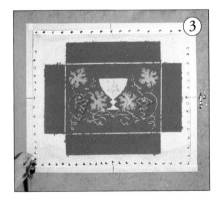

3. Stretch and secure the two sides to the board, again working from the centre out. Leave the canvas for approximately one week, or until it is completely dry.

4. Remove the canvas from the board. Trim away surplus canvas, leaving a seam allowance of approximately 3cm ($1^1/_4$in). Do not cut into the corners.

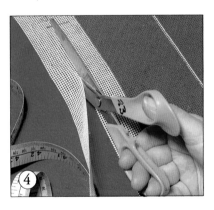

Making up

The careful making up of a kneeler will improve its appearance and lengthen its life.

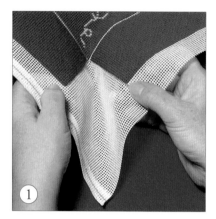

1. Match the sides at the corners, with right sides together.

2. Stitch the sides together on the wrong side, making sure that no canvas is visible on the right side. Use a small, neat back stitch along the edge of the embroidery. Do not trim the seams.

3. Turn the canvas to the right side. Create a neat box shape by pinching the top edge of the kneeler along the two empty threads of canvas and working a firm row of long-armed cross stitch around each side.

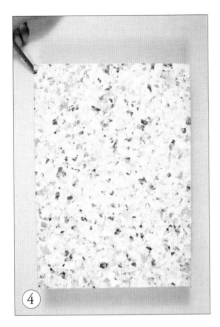

4. Place the block of foam in the centre of the piece of calico. Draw around the foam with a pencil, then put it to one side.

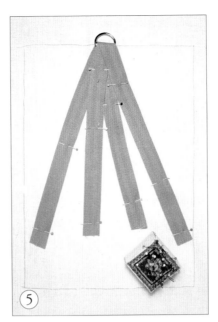

5. Cut the webbing into one length of 62cm (24in) and one of 56cm (22in). Thread the webbing through the D-ring, then splay it out so that the short lengths are on the inside. Arrange the webbing within the rectangle marked on the calico and pin it in place.

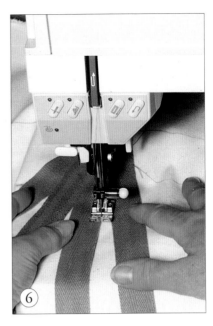

6. Sew the webbing and the D-ring on to the calico. You can either use a sewing machine, or you can do it by hand.

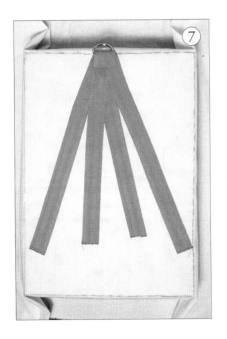

7. Place the calico over the foam block, using your pencil line as a guide. Make it up into a neat parcel by folding in the corners, pinning them in place and then hand-stitching them.

8. Cut out a piece of domette the same size as the base of the cushion. Fold the four triangles of canvas in each corner towards the narrow side of the kneeler. Place the domette at the bottom of the upturned kneeler.

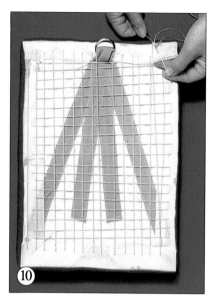

9. Drop the calico parcel into the kneeler.

10. Work lacing stitch down the length of the kneeler using upholsterer's lacing thread. Space each stitch approximately 1cm (1/2in) apart.

11. Turn the kneeler over and place the hessian centrally on top. Turn the edges of the hessian under so that it fits the kneeler. Pin the two long sides and then the two short sides in place. Mitre the corners as you come to them.

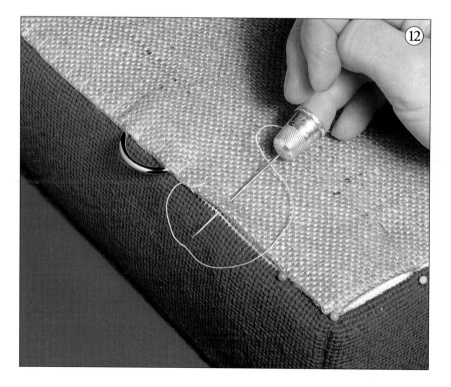

12. Sew the hessian on to the kneeler. Work in blanket stitch using a sharp, very strong needle and extra-strong thread. If you prefer an invisible join, you could use a curved needle and slip stitch.

The finished wheat and vine kneeler

This kneeler was designed by Angela Dewar and embroidered by Ann Bains, Beatrice Perry and members of Tonbridge Parish Church Sewing Group. It is worked on a twelve-thread canvas using two strands of Paterna Persian wool, with highlights in Anchor stranded cotton.

The design is particularly suitable for beginners to work, but it could be adapted to create a more challenging and exciting project. The background colour could be altered to fit into an existing scheme, and the colours in the design could also be changed: the leaves could be in autumnal shades, the chalice could be silver-grey, and the grapes green. The background is worked in diagonal tent stitch, but you could use any suitable grounding pattern, providing it does not consist of long threads lying on the surface, as these will not stand up to constant wear. You could also experiment with using small Rhodes stitches or upright cross stitch on the chalice, in place of tent stitch to add more texture. The sides of the kneeler could also be enriched by adding a border pattern.

Gallery

Kneelers from St Dunstan's Church, Mayfield, Sussex

An early archbishop of Canterbury, St Dunstan, was a man of many talents and he is surrounded by legend in Sussex and Kent. In Mayfield, the kneelers in St Dunstan's Church are designed around the stories of the saint and also around the church activities. These beautiful kneelers are full of interest and charm and are linked both by their colour and by the borders which surround each picture.

All these kneelers were designed by Anne Adam and Gillian Elvy and worked in Appleton's crewel wool using a wide variety of stitches. Members of the congregation stitched the kneelers.

TOP, LEFT TO RIGHT

This mitre design originated from a stained glass window picture of St Dunstan in St Michael and All Angel's Church in Berwick, Sussex.

Bells are still rung at St Dunstan's, which inspired the design for this kneeler. It was worked by Amanda Shaw.

The church has a musical history, especially early music, and is home to a thriving music festival. This kneeler was worked by Donald Shaw.

BOTTOM, LEFT TO RIGHT

The dove on this kneeler was taken from a design by Pat Cross which is featured on the altar cloth in the church.

This kneeler features the Coronation Crown of King Edgar, which was designed and made by St Dunstan when he was Archbishop of Canterbury.

The chalice is the symbol for St Dunstan, who was the patron saint of goldsmiths, and also a goldsmith himself. This kneeler features an ornate chalice, adapted from a Pugin design. The kneeler was stitched by Donald Shaw.

The Galilee Chapel is the Lady Chapel of Durham Cathedral and was built by Bishop Hugh du Puiset in 1175. It is remarkable for its slender marble pillars, the abundance of natural light and the twelfth-century frescoes. The kneelers at the altar rails reflect these characteristics, and are inspired by the medieval fresco in the soffit of the arch above the altar. They were designed by the Reverend Leonard Childs and worked by members of the Cathedral Broderer's Guild. A great variety of stitches has been used including satin, cushion, long-legged cross, Hungarian, woven wheel, Gobelin, tent, padded satin, Parisian and whipped back stitch.

A detail taken from one of the kneelers shown above, depicting the leaf-shaped section of the design and featuring part of the fleur-de-lys stitched in tent, woven wheel, Smyrna cross and whipped back stitch.

Photograph by Doctor Ken Nott

This Maundy Cushion from Birmingham Cathedral forms part of a set of clergy stall cushions, each with an appropriate crest for the occupier. The motif of the boat is the crest of the Lord High Almoner and the colours used in the design are based on those in the Burne Jones window shown left. The cushion was designed by Jennifer Stuart and worked by Joan Botteley on a sixteen-thread German canvas in two and three strands of Appleton's wool. Stitches used include tent, satin, upright Gobelin, cross and mosaic stitch.

Photograph by Jennifer Stuart

A Burne Jones stained glass window at Birmingham Cathedral which inspired the colours for the Maundy Cushions, one of which is shown above.

Kneelers from St Nicholas' Church, Sevenoaks, Kent

Deer from Knole Park in Sevenoaks, Kent, form the theme for this kneeler.
They are both worked in tent stitch.

In 1994, St Nicholas' Church in Sevenoaks, Kent, completed an enormous reordering scheme within the medieval church building. As part of the project, the whole of the sanctuary area was extended forward into a large, semicircular, slightly raised platform, with a splendid design of marble inlay (see page 16).

Gisela Banbury and I designed an ambitious scheme to make fifteen kneelers, all of them at least 1.5m (5ft) long, for the steps which go around the whole area. An enthusiastic team of embroiderers embarked on the task, and within less than two years the first seven kneelers were in place.

The designs for the semicircular front are based on local themes. The sides of all the kneelers feature borders of either oak leaves or acorns, and the backgrounds incorporate a pattern of oak leaves.

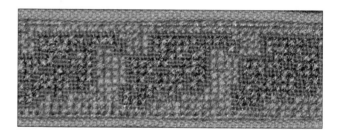

Colours for the scheme were chosen to complement the new upholstery of the seating in the church and also the marble floor of the sanctuary. This limitation of colour has the effect of adding harmony and tranquillity to an area where these things are important. Appleton's crewel wool is used throughout the scheme. The background stitch is cross stitch, chosen for its suitability for embroiderers of a range of abilities. Colours were mixed in the needle to create a tweed effect. The workers were encouraged to use other stitches wherever possible to create interest and texture.

LEFT AND ABOVE

Acorn and oak leaf borders from kneelers at St Nicholas' Church, Sevenoaks, Kent. They are both worked in cross and tent stitch.

Using Knole House in Sevenoaks, Kent, as a theme, this kneeler is worked in a variety of stitches to create the impression of stone walls. Different colours have been mixed in the needle to add texture to the embroidery.

This attractive kneeler shows a view of one of the buildings of Sevenoaks School in Kent. The building is worked in upright Gobelin and tent stitch is used for the windows.

The famous seven oaks in Kent, which gave the town its name, feature in the background of this kneeler. The foreground shows an ancient cricketer playing on the Vine Ground. The trees are worked in shaded leaf stitch.

These charming kneelers from St Bartholomew's Church in Burwash, Sussex, feature a pair of birds, designed by the late Barbara Newton and worked by Elsie Taylor; and a partridge in a pear tree, designed and stitched by Peta Longstaff. Both kneelers are worked in tent stitch, back stitch, cross stitch, rice stitch and Gobelin.

*These two kneelers, both from St Bartholomew's Church in Burwash, Sussex, feature an
impressive local house, designed by the late Barbara Newton and worked by Alice Ransom; and
the village shop, designed by the late Barbara Newton and worked by Elsie Taylor. Both kneelers
are worked in tent stitch and cross stitch.*

These kneelers are from St Augustine's Chapel, Tonbridge School, Kent, and are designed by Donald Buttress MA Dip Arch RIBA FSA, who redesigned the chapel interior after a disastrous fire in 1988. They have been interpreted by Pam Rawson-Mackenzie and Sara Stonor, stitched by parents and friends and made up by Gilly Cowan and her team. Stitches include Gobelin, rice, satin stitch square, tent, cashmere and Florentine stitch.

These colourful and exciting kneelers were designed by Barbara Warren for St John the Evangelist's Church in Hildenborough, Kent. They were worked by members of the congregation using cross stitch.

43

These pew kneelers form part of a set designed for St Peter and St Paul's Church in Tonbridge, Kent. The kneelers are linked by the common feature of the Pugin floor tiles pattern, and all are stitched in tent stitch and single cross.

CLOCKWISE FROM TOP LEFT

The Reverend Jane Austin chose a musical theme for her design for this memorial kneeler.

This kneeler features symbols of St Peter and St Paul, and is designed and worked by Beatrice Perry.

This heraldic design represents the family of the novelist Jane Austen, who had connections with the parish. The motifs in the shield are the paws of a bear. The kneeler is designed and worked by Beatrice Perry.

The ship is a symbol for the Church. This kneeler was designed by Beatrice Perry and worked by Christine Hoather.

This picture shows a pair of matching stool kneelers from St Nicholas' Church in Sevenoaks, Kent. They are worked by Bill Salter, Joan Miller and Eileen Wrighton. The designer chose the same colours as used in the main scheme and these kneelers are used in the sanctuary. The stool kneeler at the bottom of the picture is from St John's Methodist Church, Southborough, Kent. An all-over pattern of satin and tent stitch is worked in Appleton's crewel wool by the late Margaret Herbert.

This kneeler was designed for the bishop's throne in St James' Church in Hartlebury, Worcestershire. It is one of a set designed and worked by Jennifer Stuart and the Hartlebury Church Needleworkers. The colours are chosen to match the paintwork on the ribs of the ceiling vaulting and to blend with the carpeting and Victorian floor tiles. The shell design is the symbol of St James and also of Pilgrims. The kneeler is worked on a natural plain weave canvas and mainly uses two strands of Appleton's crewel wool. The sides are covered in a furnishing velvet. Stitches include long-armed cross, padded satin, tent, Rhodes and rice stitch.

LEFT

These two kneelers are from a large set at St Mary's Church in Speldhurst, Kent. The kneeler at the top of the picture features a rose, which is one of the flowers associated with the Virgin. The kneeler is worked in cross stitch, using tapestry wool, and is designed by Jane Ellison and made by Enid Birling. The kneeler at the bottom of the picture features a design taken from one of the original twelfth-century tiles found around the altar and shows the staff of St Christopher with two mocking birds. The kneeler is worked in cross stitch and is designed and made by Jane Ellison.

RIGHT

These four kneelers were designed for St John the Baptist's Church in Penshurst, Kent by the late Miss Clements. It is a beautiful country church in an attractive village, and the simple pattern of English wild flowers is appropriate for the setting. The kneelers are worked in tent and cross stitch.

LEFT

This wedding kneeler was designed by Angela Dewar and worked by Sheila Hoole. It is stitched with Paterna Persian wool using a variety of stitches, including leaf stitch, satin stitch square and Gobelin.

A pair of wedding kneelers from St Bartholomew's Church, Burwash, Sussex. The kneelers are designed by Anna Pearson and worked in a wide variety of stitches and yarns by Margot Sanderson and Sara Stonor.

Index

This kneeler was designed by Angela Dewar for St John's Methodist Church, Southborough, Kent. It occupies an end position as indicated by the free border design. It is worked by Elaine Vonberg and stitched in Appleton's crewel wool, using tent, Gobelin and velvet stitch.